ADAPTED TO SURVIVE

ANIMALS THAT FLY

Angela Royston

Raintree is an imprint of Capstone Global Library Limited, a company incorporated in England and Wales having its registered office at 7 Pilgrim Street, London, EC4V 6LB – Registered company number: 6695582

www.raintreepublishers.co.uk
myorders@raintreepublishers.co.uk

Text © Capstone Global Library Limited 2014
First published in hardback in 2014
The moral rights of the proprietor have been asserted.

Edited by Dan Nunn, Rebecca Rissman, and Helen Cox Cannons
Designed by Jo Hinton-Malivoire
Picture research by Mica Brancic
Originated by Capstone Global Library Ltd
Production by Helen McCreath
Printed and bound in China

ISBN 978 1 406 27084 6
17 16 15 14 13
10 9 8 7 6 5 4 3 2 1

British Library Cataloguing in Publication Data
A full catalogue record for this book is available from the British Library.

Acknowledgements
We would like to thank the following for permission to reproduce photographs: Naturepl.com pp. 4 (© John Abbott), 5 (© Ian McCarthy), 6 (© Peter Blackwell), 8 (© Bernard Castelein), 9 (© Edwin Giesbers), 11 (Geslin/© Wild Wonders of Europe), 12 (© Kevin Schafer), 13 (© Barry Mansell), 14 (Maitland/© Wild Wonders of Europe), 15, 26 (© Stephen Dalton), 16 (© Rolf Nussbaumer), 17 (© David Tipling), 18 (© Philip Dalton), 19 (© Nick Upton), 21 (© Tui De Roy), 22, 29 bottom right (© Brent Stephenson), 23 (© David Fleetham), 25 (© Kim Taylor), 27 (© Tim Laman); Science Photo Library p. 10 (Steve Gschmeissner); Shutterstock pp. 7 (© Igor Kovalenko), 20 (© Christian Musat), 29 top right (© Rob van Esch), 29 top left (© niceregionpics), 24, 29 bottom left (Minden Pictures).

Cover photograph of a Grey heron flying reproduced with permission of Shutterstock (© Neal Cooper).

We would like to thank Michael Bright for his invaluable help in the preparation of this book.

Every effort has been made to contact copyright holders of material reproduced in this book. Any omissions will be rectified in subsequent printings if notice is given to the publisher.

Disclaimer
All the internet addresses (URLs) given in this book were valid at the time of going to press. However, due to the dynamic nature of the internet, some addresses may have changed, or sites may have changed or ceased to exist since publication. While the author and publisher regret any inconvenience this may cause readers, no responsibility for any such changes can be accepted by either the author or the publisher.

Some words are shown in bold, **like this.** You can find out what they mean by looking in the glossary.

CONTENTS

WHICH ANIMALS FLY?

Birds and insects are the most common flying animals. Bats can also fly. Some animals, including fish, can **glide**! Why and how do animals fly?

beetle

Largest flying birds

The wandering albatross has the largest **wingspan** of all birds. Its wingspan can reach 3½ metres (11 feet) across.

WHY ANIMALS FLY

Animals fly for several reasons. Flying is a good way of getting from one place to another. Birds and insects fly away from danger on the ground. Insects fly from flower to flower to find food, and some birds catch insects as they fly.

This lion is trying to grab a vulture before it can fly away.

DID YOU KNOW?
Snow geese avoid the cold Arctic winter by flying south to a warmer country.

ADAPTED TO FLY

Adaptations are special things about an animal's body that help it to **survive**. Flying animals have wings that lift and push them through the air. Birds and bats have strong wings made of bones, covered with feathers or skin. The wing bones are the same bones that form our arms and fingers.

Insect wings are made of very thin skin.

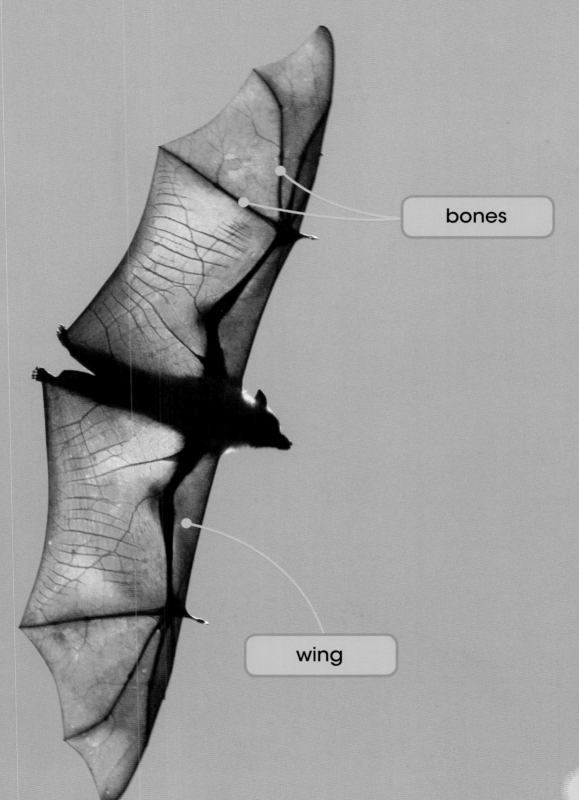

bones

wing

BIRD CHAMPIONS

As well as wings, birds have other **adaptations** that help them to fly. Their bones and feathers are hollow, which makes them strong and light. Swifts can fly amazingly fast – at 112 kilometres (69 miles) per hour.

hollow bird bone

peregrine falcon diving

Peregrine falcons can dive at a speed of around 320 kilometres (200 miles) per hour.

BATS

A bat can change the shape of its wing as it flies. This allows the bat to change direction very fast. Bats find their way in the dark by making high-pitched squeaks and listening for the echoes. This **adaptation** is called echolocation.

DID YOU KNOW?
Bats hang upside down to sleep.

INSECTS

Most insects have two pairs of wings, which they beat very fast. Insects can quickly take off in any direction to escape from danger. Insects are so small that it is hard to measure exactly how fast they can fly. Desert locusts are probably the fastest fliers, at 33 kilometres (20 miles) per hour.

owlfly

dragonfly

HOVERING

Some birds can **hover**, or stay still in mid-air like a helicopter. Hummingbirds beat their wings very fast and hover while they sip **nectar** from flowers. **Birds of prey** hover, too. They fly into the wind and use their wings to stay in the same place.

Kites watch out for **prey** on the
ground and then they dive to grab it!

HOVERING INSECTS

Some insects, such as hoverflies, can **hover**, too. Hummingbird hawkmoths hover like hummingbirds to feed from flowers. They have a long **proboscis**, which they use like a straw. This **adaptation** allows them to suck **nectar** from tube-shaped flowers.

proboscis

19

GLIDING

Birds **glide** when they move through the air without flapping their wings. Gliding takes less energy than flying, so large birds often glide. For example, albatrosses, vultures, eagles, and storks are good gliders.

Birds that glide have long, large wings.

stork

condor

Ace glider
A condor uses rising warm air to help it glide. It may flap its wings only once every hour to keep going.

FLYING FISH

Flying fish have large side **fins** that act like wings. The fish leap out of the water and **glide** to escape from ocean **predators**. A flying fish can glide for up to 45 seconds and cover up to 400 metres (1,312 feet).

Amazing fish

A flying fish pushes its tail against the water as it drops down. This helps it to lift up again.

FLYING SQUIRRELS

Flying squirrels live in trees. They have a large flap of furry skin between the front and back legs on each side of their bodies. This **adaptation** allows them to **glide** from tree to tree. A flying squirrel uses its flat tail to help itself steer.

A flying squirrel thrusts its feet forwards to slow itself down before it lands.

FLYING DRAGONS

A flying dragon is a lizard that lives in trees. Its "wings" are flaps of skin attached to extra-long **rib** bones on each side of its body. It can **glide** for up to 9 metres (30 feet) from one tree to another. It uses its tail to help it steer.

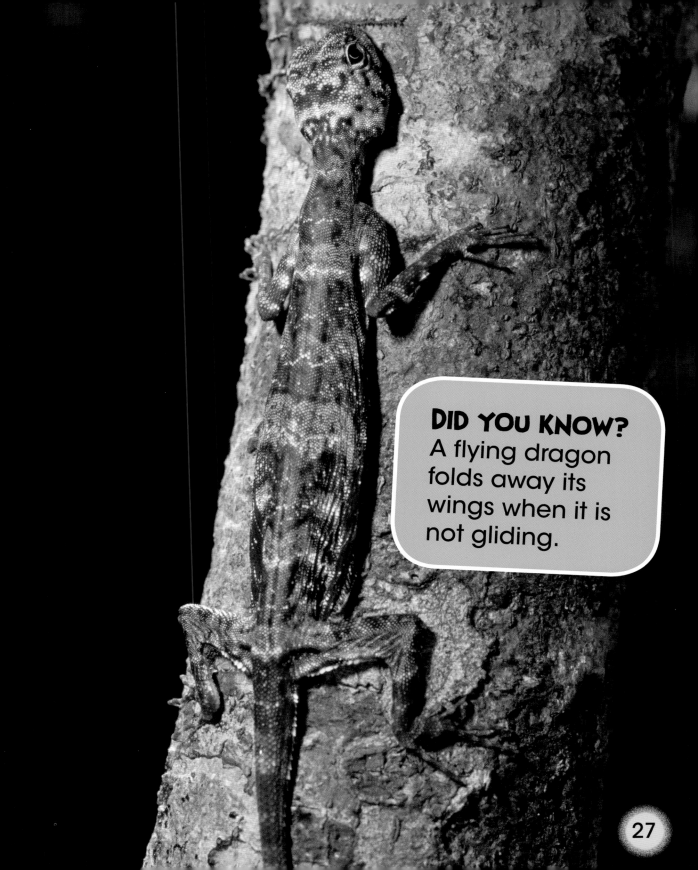

DID YOU KNOW?
A flying dragon folds away its wings when it is not gliding.

ANIMAL CHALLENGE

1. Do you think small wings or big wings are better for flying long distances?

2. Cats climb trees, but do not **glide**. What **adaptation** would they need to glide?

3. Why can't penguins fly through the air?

Invent your own flying animal. You can use some of the adaptations shown in the photos or make up your own.

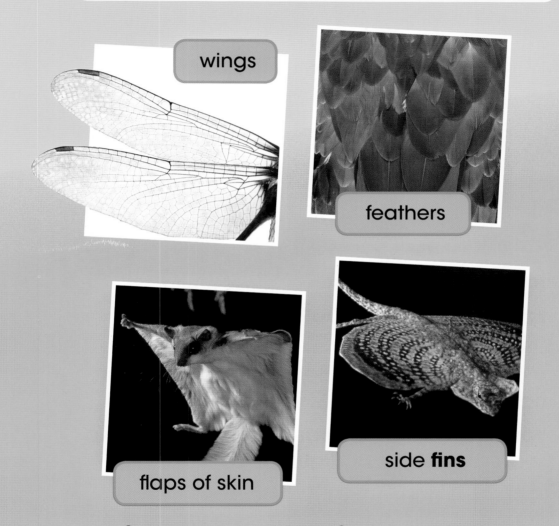

wings

feathers

flaps of skin

side **fins**

Answers to Animal Challenge

1. Big wings are better for flying long distances, because they provide more lift.
2. In order to glide, one adaptation that would help a cat would be to have flaps of skin that stretch between the front and back legs.
3. A penguin is too heavy and its wings are too small for it to fly through the air. Instead, it uses its wings as flippers to swim through the water.

GLOSSARY

adaptation special thing about an animal's body that helps it to survive in a particular way or in a particular habitat

bird of prey bird that hunts and eats small animals, such as mice and other birds

fins stiff flaps that stick out from a fish's body to help the fish move and steer

glide to move through the air without flapping wings

hover to hang in the air without moving forwards or backwards

nectar sweet juice made inside some flowers

predator animal that hunts and kills other animals for food

prey animal that is hunted and eaten by another animal

proboscis long tube through which an insect or other animal sucks up liquid

rib one of a number of curved bones that protect the heart of an animal

survive manage to go on living

wingspan distance from one wingtip to the other when the wings are stretched open

FIND OUT MORE

BOOKS

Bats, Megan Cullis (Usborne, 2009)

Birds, Gill Doherty (Usborne, 2008)

RSPB First Book of Birds, Anita Ganeri and David Chandler (A & C Black, 2011)

WEBSITES

www.bats.org.uk/pages/all_about_bats.html
The website of the Bat Conservation Trust explains echolocation and gives lots of information about bats.

www.bbc.co.uk/nature/life/Macroglossum_stellatarum
Short videos and text on this website show you how hummingbird hawkmoths hover and feed.

www.rspb.org.uk/youth/learn/adaptation/flight/index.aspx
The website for the Royal Society for the Protection of Birds includes a section on adaptation.

INDEX